THE
25 IMMUTABLE RULES
OF SUCCESSFUL TOURISM

ROGER A. BROOKS
& MAURY FORMAN

KENDALL/HUNT PUBLISHING COMPANY
4050 Westmark Drive   Dubuque, Iowa 52002

"Nothing great was ever accomplished without enthusiasm."
- Ralph Waldo Emerson

Cover photo courtesy of Washington State Office of Business & Tourism Development. Rafting on the Snoqualmie River with Mt. Si in the background, near North Bend, WA. Inside cover photo: The spectacular Oregon Coast. Photo this page: Fly fishing in Central Oregon.

Contents

Acknowledgments

There may be 25 immutable rules for tourism, but there is only one immutable rule in writing a book. It is the rule of thanks. There are a number of people who have helped us with this book in doing research, coming up with ideas, and with the actual writing. Writing a book is similar to planning a trip. It is usually a group effort, and this book would never have come together if it had not been for a number of people.

We are very grateful for the excellent input and editing of this book by Lindy Hoppough, Director of Editorial Services for Chabin Concepts in Chico, CA. Her keen eye for details helped make the book more readable and practical for communities interested in further developing their tourism industry. Our appreciation also goes out to Lisa Cosmillo of the Thurston County Economic Development Organization in Olympia, Washington and Betsy Gilder of the Lodi Community Library in Lodi, Ohio. Brainstorming ideas with them helped make writing this publication an enjoyable process.

We would like to thank Martha Choe, Director of the Washington State Department of Community, Trade and Economic Development (CTED); Robin Pollard, Assistant Director for Economic Development, CTED; Peter McMillin, Managing Director for Business and Tourism Development, CTED; and Linda Alongi, Education and Training Coordinator, CTED, for their support of this project. They provide continued assistance for educational tools such as this book, knowing that education and training is part of developing a successful economic development program.

The 25 Immutable Rules of Tourism was introduced at the nationally recognized Northwest Economic Development Games in Ellensburg, Washington in 1996, as a two-hour multi-media workshop. Since that time, this presentation has been seen in hundreds of communities throughout the country and often followed by an in-depth and practical community assessment. The team at Destination Development deserves a lot of credit for years of research, finding anecdotal stories and case histories from around the world. Thanks especially to Rebecca Durkin and Jane Brooks for their unwavering support in getting this book out.

And finally, we'd like to thank Cheryl Rasch, Business and Tourism Development, CTED, for her assistance in securing some excellent photography from the state's tourism website www.experiencewashington.com.

For more information visit www.destinationdevelopment.com

Introduction

What is it that can take months to plan yet is often over in just a few days or weeks; can be done in a car, train, boat or plane; may cost a whole lot or very little; requires little (or sometimes nothing) in the way of clothing; and almost always brings people and even nations together?

The answer, of course, is travel. Whether for business, pleasure or rest and relaxation, travel is the most coveted and sought after activity in the world. The average traveler takes time away from everyday life and the stresses of work and home to expend time and money attempting to avoid stress elsewhere—hence the popular term "getaway." Done well, travel —especially vacationing—is an indispensable part of our lives. But if your "family vacations" are like the cinematic character Clark Griswold in National Lampoon's *Vacation*, it may be an oxymoron. Chevy Chase plays the hapless suburbanite from Chicago, traveling with his family across America looking for fun and relaxation. And although everything is planned, nothing goes right. The family endures wrong turns, misleading promotions, rude employees, multiple parking tickets, and unwanted relatives. Yet nothing deters Clark Griswold from spending two memorable weeks with his wife and kids.

And apparently, he's not alone. The family vacation has made a long-awaited comeback, although in an altered state. Families are traveling in cars and RVs more than planes; they have switched from two-week trips to multiple, extended, weekend jaunts; they are discovering attractions in their own back yards; they are choosing to avoid many of the entertaining destinations and are rediscovering their heritage and the arts; they are staying more often with family and friends; and they are looking for things to do rather than things to buy. And they are spending a lot more money in the process.

Tourism is quickly becoming the "industry of choice" in many communities, while in others it has become "the industry because we have no other choice." Thousands of communities, particularly in rural areas across North America, have seen drastic cutbacks in the industries on which they were founded. Mining, agriculture, fishing, and timber are just a few that have seen dramatic cutbacks and closures

over the past twenty years. As a result, nearly every community, big or small, is looking to diversify—and tourism seems to be the most natural and easiest diversification strategy.

Tourism As an Economic Development Strategy

Less than a decade ago, cities and towns never considered tourism as an "economic development strategy." Yet today, thousands are developing and promoting the industry and see it as a vital part of their economies. The benefit behind tourism is to "import" more cash into your community than you "export." When you earn money in your town and spend some of it elsewhere, it's referred to as "leakage." Communities with a successful tourism industry import more cash than they export. Results have shown that tourism can bring substantial benefits to a community and its residents. For example, tourism:

• Diversifies the economy so that communities are no longer dependent on one or two industries.

• Provides a multiplier effect where many businesses, including non-tourism industries, benefit economically.

• Brings in "new money" that creates growth in a community.

• Increases the tax base that helps pay for community amenities and services.

• Creates jobs and business opportunities for entry level people and entrepreneurs.

• Promotes business development. Today's visitor may just be tomorrow's investor—something seen more and more, particularly in the rural areas.

• Boosts appearance and makes the community visually appealing.

Tourism is often an intangible industry with regards to quantifying its true economic benefit. Yet travel and tourism, in the U.S. alone, generates $555 billion in annual visitor spending (2001), and employs 7.9 million workers with an annual payroll of $174 billion. If economic development is about creating

When people who live and work in your community spend some of that money in other areas, it's referred to as "leakage." Tourism is the number one method to recapture that loss. After all, visitors come, they play, they spend, then go home. Successful tourism happens when you import more money than you export. Successful communities are subsidized by visitors, as opposed to subsidizing visitors. Which category do you fall under?

community wealth, then tourism should be considered a very important strategy for every community. Are you seeing your fair share of these revenues and jobs?

What Are These "Immutable Rules"?

The Immutable Rules you are about to read are a collection of suggestions every community should consider to help draw visitors and their cash to the area. While travel is flexible, the immutable rules aren't. As a matter of fact, the rules are *immutable* because they *don't* change, and communities that implement them see continued success.

The 25 rules in this book are designed to provide simple ways to make tourism a profitable undertaking by attracting the right kind of visitor and getting them to stay longer, which translates to additional spending. The more the visitor spends in your community, the less you, the local resident, will have to pay for better streets, law enforcement, and public amenities that you can enjoy every day.

In order to be successful in your tourism efforts:
1. You must be able to get passers-by to stop.

2. You need to create ways to keep them in town longer—translating to additional spending.

3. You will want to work towards becoming the overnight or multi-day destination. After all, overnight visitors spend three times that of day visitors, and infinitely more than pass-through visitors.

As you will see, the focus of these rules is not just about getting more visitors into your community, but in encouraging them to stay longer. The longer they stay, the more they will spend. The more you apply these rules, the more successful you will be.

Are You Looking for Tourists or Visitors?

If increasing tourism in your community is part of your plans, perhaps we should define what a "tourist" is. The traditional meaning of tourist is a person traveling away from home for leisure purposes. The tourism industry usually considers anyone traveling at least fifty miles from home—for any purpose—a tourist. If someone comes into your town from out of town, that person is a "tourist."

We actually prefer using the word "visitor," because "tourist" implies only the leisure traveler. Visitors include business travelers as well. After all, business travel is a primary source of imported dollars for communities. Therefore, when we refer to "visitors" in this book, we are including people visiting friends and family, business travelers, convention and trade show attendees, passers-by simply stopping for gas and/or food, parents visiting kids in college, and the occasional visitor who is just visiting your community to have a good time.

To the visitor, a vacation is a way to create memories. The Clark Griswolds of the world will remember the time they spent with friends and family, the destinations they visited, the experiences they shared, and the items they bought. The trip really had no rules other than to have fun together. But to the community, the Griswold's experience required following a set of rules that will keep them coming back again and again. It costs a whole lot less to bring visitors back again than to keep getting new ones.

Questions for Success:

- Have you developed a "business plan" for tourism development and marketing?
- Do you really know who your customers are and why they visit you?
- Do you have a coordinated tourism effort?
- Does your tourism program tie to your economic development programs?
- Is there continuity in your marketing messages, materials and marketing theme?
- Are you seeing a good return on your investment in your tourism marketing and development efforts?
- Have you developed a plan with a good balance of product development and marketing?

Rule I

SUCCESS BEGINS WITH A GOOD ARCHITECT

The rule of planning

Can you imagine building your dream home without a set of plans? The result would be a quirky set of misaligned walls and stairs leading nowhere, perhaps suitable as a tourist attraction in its own right, but not that livable.

In fact, that's just what the wealthy heiress, Sarah Winchester, did in San Jose, California. To foil evil spirits, she continually built onto her existing mansion. There are 2,000 doors (that's an average of twelve per room), forty staircases, and numerous secret passages. It is so complex, that even the mistress of the manor required a map to get around. And after her death, the Winchester Mystery House did indeed become a popular tourist attraction.

Winchester House is the exception to the rule; most communities do not wish to be known for their lack of planning. Too many communities use the shotgun approach: "Let's run an ad here, let's send a press release there, we need another sign over there...." Without any continuity, you just cannot build an industry that will stand the test of time.

As a community, you need to bring together your partners to plan what type of tourism activities will bring outside dollars into the area. The outcome of this process will be your Tourism Development & Marketing Plan—a blueprint that every community should have. It will include strategies for both product development and marketing. It will encompass every rule in this book. This "Action Plan" should be so detailed, that anyone can follow its recommendations and build a thriving tourism industry in the community.

People can be attracted to your community by any of four different features:
• Natural resources (lakes, forests, wildlife, recreation)
• Cultural resources (history, cuisine, ethnic)
• Human resources (performing arts, craftsmen, artisans)
• Capital resources (transportation, hotels, utilities)

Understanding the types of resources that are available and how they best fit into the overall plan is critical in getting your community on someone's radar.

After a community identifies what it has that sets it apart from everyone else, finding out who to target becomes a little easier. Tourism plans must target different types of attractions to different types of visitors. There are day visitors, convention attendees, business travelers, people visiting friends and family, vacationers, and niche groups from bird watchers to motorcycle clubs. They all spend money when they come to town. But they all want different services and amenities to cater to their particular needs and desires.

Approach your tourism plan as if you were designing a house. It should feature a welcoming entryway, all the necessary amenities such as bathrooms, a place to play, a place to relax, and a special room for each of your guests. You certainly don't want your community on the list of condemned places to avoid. If only Sarah Winchester had known: planning is the best method to keep the evil spirits at bay.

QUESTIONS FOR SUCCESS:
- Have you developed partnerships that include both public and private attractions?
- Is everyone on the same page in terms of your branding effort?
- Is there continuity in your tourism marketing and development efforts?
- Are you working closely with state agencies and taking advantage of other available resources?

What kind of "ship" never sails alone?

If you answered partnership, then you have just recognized the most important rule in creating a successful tourism strategy. Partners are so important, that it is impossible to even think that tourism programs can be successful when executed by a single entity. Take San Diego, California. By partnering with an assortment of attractions—San Diego Zoo, SeaWorld, and even Disneyland, which is about ninety-five miles to the north—San Diego presents itself as part of the larger Southern California experience, worth traveling a longer distance to visit, and thus convincing millions of visitors to stay for a longer period of time.

In most communities, there is typically a single lead agency that coordinates tourism development, promotion, activities, and events. It may be a visitors bureau or the local chamber of commerce. But just because they are leading the charge, this does not mean they should do it alone. Tourism development and promotion must be a team sport—especially in smaller communities where resources are limited.

Partnerships accomplish a number of goals: they create continuity in the marketing effort, build a stronger brand for the community, reduce the duplication of efforts (multiple websites, toll-free numbers, etc.), and make "selling" the community easier. Prospective visitors are more likely to act when presented with a single vision, a single contact, and a single source for getting initial information.

There are three types of tourism partnerships, and all three should be developed. First, there are financial partnerships with other communities or tourism promoters, in which one or all of the partners pool funds to accomplish certain tourism objectives. This allows communities to leverage available funds for discounts on advertising, the hiring of public relations services, development of quality photo libraries, and quality website development.

The second type of partnership involves shared resources, which also avoids the common duplication of services and visitor confusion. Imagine the benefit of shared photo libraries and press kits, single toll-free information request lines, etc.

The third type of partnership involves leveraging the dollars and resources with private sector businesses. Quite often, the best attractions are privately owned. Work with them. Bring them into the program. Create "public/private partnerships." Look at what San Diego has done.

Partners involved in tourism should include economic development organizations, convention centers, chambers of commerce, tribal units, cultural attractions and organizations, and event organizers, as well as city, state, or federal agencies. The more partners you have, the more successful you will be. The biggest partnerships should be between communities, counties, or regions. You'll always be much more successful as one loud voice, rather than a bunch of small voices.

Recently, the Washington State Audubon Society, a nonprofit organization, teamed up with three state agencies—Trade and Economic Development, Fish and Wildlife, and Department of Transportation—six communities, and the Bullet Foundation. Each organization had a role in providing technical, professional, or financial support. The final result was the creation of the first Great Washington State Birding Trail.

Tourism partnerships are very much like a marriage. You agree, disagree, get upset, compromise, and then move on to a decision that will make all parties reasonably happy. The only difference is that in tourism, it's perfectly legal to have multiple partners—especially when you are building partnerships.

While the billboard (top) is attractive, does it entice you to take the next exit? Does the event listed sell you on making a special trip back to Lovelock for Frontier Days? In promoting its casino gaming, Winnemucca played off the legend of Butch Cassidy who purportedly spent time in Winnemucca. The billboard provides a great teaser that will peak interest, is easy to read, has only nine words, and simple graphics. Billboards must tell visitors WHY they should visit you.

When people go fishing, they know that if they want to catch fish, they have to bring the right bait. Whether it's a distant shining object or a tasty wriggling morsel, something must entice the fish to take notice and say, "Now that looks intriguing."

People are not that different from fish. They need to be lured into your community. Billboards, highway signage, and other "teasers" are your bait.

Signs along the highway are most effective when they offer uncommitted visitors something they want. It may be food, an attraction, an event, or even "the facilities." One of the biggest mistakes that communities make is not telling visitors *why* they should visit. Billboards should focus on activities— things to do. After all, people go places to do things.

The traveler may not even know what they want until they see the "teaser" or information while driving past. But without that information sitting on that lonely road, no one is going to know that there is anything to do if they take your exit. "Give me a reason."

In order to be effective, highway signs must be presented in an eye-catching manner. There are four keys to success: Use the right words, make it brief, keep the design simple, and keep the sign well maintained.

Strong action words are the most successful draws to a community. Avoid worn-out or meaningless words like "welcome," "discover," "explore," or "we have it all." These signs seldom work because they don't give the visitor a reason to stop. You can only "discover" something once. The goal of your community is to keep people coming back time and again.

Promoting yourself as a "gateway" is overused and used incorrectly. Gateways are something you drive through to get somewhere else. You want to be that somewhere else.

Make sure your highway signs are brief. People traveling at highway speeds will have approximately four seconds to read your message. If it's too much to read or too cluttered, the average traveler will simply ignore the sign. Have you ever turned to the person sitting next to you and asked, "could you read all that?" or "what did that say?" The most effective signs will include fewer than fourteen words. The best ones use fewer than ten. Fish won't bite if you hang half a dozen lures on the same line. In fact, they'll make a point of staying away.

Keep your signage and graphics simple. Most photos and graphic images are difficult to absorb from a distance. If a traveler has to spend all four seconds making out the graphic or photo, you've lost them. Magazine-style ads never make good billboards.

Finally, make sure that people or organizations are assigned the responsibility of maintaining and updating the signage. Weeds and grass grow high when left unattended, and crucial information is often blocked from the view of speeding motorists. Do not expect the highway department to do this. There is also no reason for motorists to stop when signage informs people of an event that has already taken place. Highways are a community's front door, and you want to welcome people with a well-manicured entrance and current promotion of your activities—a good first impression.

Like fish, your potential visitors will be enticed by eye-catching bait that is too tempting to pass up. Additionally, they won't bite at all, unless you drop your line where the fish are swimming. In the case of tourism, this means out on the highways.

Questions for Success:

- Do you have restroom facilities available to visitors?
- If so, do you have signage letting them know they're available?
- Are your facilities close to places where those visitors can spend time and money?
- Are they well maintained?
- Are they easy to find?
- Is visitor information readily available?
- How do your restrooms stack up?
- Do they fairly represent your community in terms of cleanliness, curb appeal, etc?

"I gotta go." Those are the three most feared words heard by a parent on a long trip in the family car. You know it will be miles before you reach the next rest stop. It hasn't been that long since you passed the last one and asked the kids, "Do you have to go?" Of course, no one said a word. You press your foot down a little harder on the accelerator, hoping to make time pass quickly as your children begin to squirm in their seats.

Who would have ever thought that a small bladder would be such an important part of a community's tourism strategy?

Restrooms are one of the easiest devices for luring visitors into your community. After all, you never know when the urge to go will cause them to stop.

Most state highway departments won't post signs for public restrooms other than rest stops, but if communities can promote the fact that they have them, they are sure to benefit from additional visitor spending.

You'd be surprised how a billboard with the words "Clean public restrooms—easy access" can translate into visitor spending. How? After you have used the facilities, have you ever said, "While we're here, why don't we look in that shop over there." Or, "While we're here, why don't we get something to eat?"

If your public restrooms also incorporate a visitor information kiosk, or are located next to an antique store, restaurant or attraction, the "facilities" can be surprisingly effective at bringing in customers. People like to stretch their legs a bit. They like the break. You, as a community, need to take full advantage of the most basic of human needs and the number one reason passers-by make unscheduled stops.

Businesses make a big mistake when they post signs stating that restrooms are for customers only. Most people don't even think about buying anything until they come out of the restroom. They will always empty the bladder before the pocket book. Prohibitive signs discourage visitors from becoming customers.

McDonald's doesn't offer public restrooms, but it knows that its restrooms are often seen that way. Every restaurant makes a priority of keeping its restrooms clean because their use typically translates into sales.

It's simple math. Imagine seven people crammed into a van on their way to a conference. After about one hundred miles, someone squirms uncomfortably and shouts, "Take the next exit. I see a restroom!"

What the person sees are golden arches. At the McDonald's, seven people pour out of the van. A couple of them go across the street to the Chevron Mini-Mart, and the rest enter the restaurant. Fifteen minutes later, they pile back into the van relieved of $40 spent on drinks and snacks to fuel them up until the next stop.

You'd probably be surprised at the sales volume mini-marts make as customers walk past the candy aisle and drink cooler on the way to and from the "facilities." Maybe you aren't surprised because you are one of those customers.

Multiply this one van by the number of vehicles that could be taking your off-ramp every day, and it can pay for a lot of toilet paper.

Smart communities have a profitable little secret: they provide people with the thing they need the most. People need restrooms. Located close to attractions or other visitor amenities with easy highway access, toilets will attract more money than flies.

EXAMPLE:

Based on the welcome sign (above) what is your impression of Borrego Springs, California? Does it look like a community you'd want to explore or visit for several days? It just so happens that Borrego Springs is surrounded by the Anza-Borrego Desert State Park—the largest and one of the most unique parks in the nation. The community also offers several terrific golf courses, outstanding resorts (top photos), interpretive centers, and a shopping village. Often, well-meaning organizations develop these signs as volunteers without realizing the negative effect they can have—which reflects directly in

It may be true that we shouldn't judge a book by its cover, but it's also true that we all do. Think back to your first moments with this book. Before even turning a page, you were already forming expectations about the level of quality you would expect on the inside.

Each entryway into your community is the cover of your book. It provides the first hint about the character and quality of the people and businesses within your community. Make no doubt about it, your community WILL be judged by its cover.

Look at your community as a mall. You want visitors to come, spend time and money in your mall, then go home and tell friends how great it was. Wherever you have posted the first sign that states "Entering Smallville" or "Welcome to Smallville" is the entrance to your mall. Take a long look at your entrance signage, which should be decorative—not the typical aluminum street signs. Look at the landscaping, the lighting, and the businesses, or homes adjacent to the entryway.

When you're on the road and looking for a place to eat, how often have you said, "That *looks* like a nice place to eat"? If you're like the vast majority of people, you just made a judgment about the restaurant and its food by the building's general appeal and its signage. The same applies to lodging establishments, attractions, golf courses, and retail stores. As a visitor, if not recommended by someone, we make judgments based on appearance—it's the only guide we have. The first impression will ultimately result in either "This looks like a nice place to stop" or "Let's keep going while we look for something more appealing."

Here are three important rules to creating a good first impression:

• Make sure that your entrance features and entryways are placed where they will make the best first impression. Most communities place them at the city or county limits. This has little or no value as there really is no need to mark your territory. Placing them there serves very little purpose and usually paints a less-than-attractive picture of the community. Take a look at your city or county limits.

• Another common mistake that communities make is creating sign clutter at their entryways. This often includes auxiliary organization signs, listings of events, etc. Never list more than four items and keep your verbiage to a minimum. Put local auxilary signage at a separate location where visitors can stop and take note of when or where the organizations meet.

• Communities should not skimp on their welcome signs. They should be considered an investment with a tremendous return. Make sure the signs are attractive, professionally produced (sorry volunteers), impeccably landscaped with lots of color, lit at night, and cleaned and/or repainted once a year. Welcome signs and entry landscapes should be large, creating a "grand" entrance. They should be placed on both sides of the street or even span the street, if possible. Your "welcome" or "entry" should create a sense of arrival and make the visitor want to stop.

Quality entries state that you are a quality community, thereby increasing the perceived value of the area. The greater the perceived value, the more visitors will spend, and the longer they will stay. For residents, that translates into increased property values; stronger community pride; and the desire to live, work, and play in the community. A community can make an amazing and lasting impression by just putting out the welcome mat.

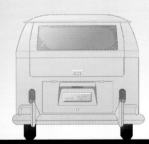

QUESTIONS FOR SUCCESS:

- How easy is it for visitors to find what you have to offer in the way of attractions, amenities, and services?
- Is your signage in keeping with the communities overall theme or ambiance?
- Is there continuity throughout the community in terms of signage?
- Do you have an ongoing signage program in place?

In 1803, President Thomas Jefferson won approval from Congress for a visionary project that was to become one of American history's greatest adventure stories. Jefferson wanted to know if Americans could journey overland to the Pacific Ocean following two rivers—the Missouri and the Columbia.

It has been 200 years since Meriwether Lewis and William Clark made their historic 8,000-mile, 28-month trip. What makes their travels even more amazing is that they did it without any signs that said, "Scenic Body of Water: This Way."

Most travelers today do not have the time or the patience to travel the lengths that Lewis and Clark did. Yet haphazard signage in some communities leads visitors into an unrecognizable wilderness, with no navigational aids to guide them. Signs should lead people to a destination, not astray.

There are two primary signage issues that are critical to the success of any community: gateways and directional (or wayfinding) signage. Gateways introduce visitors to your community and provide a sense of arrival. Directional signs help visitors navigate through the area, while telling them what there is to see and do, where amenities are located (public parking, restrooms, visitor information, local services), and where the attractions are.

Some communities have even developed color-coded signage so that visitors can identify their next destination from a distance. As an example, public amenities might be in yellow, attractions in blue, and shopping areas in green. Signs can and should promote spending in your community, and can be a very powerful and effective selling tool. Developing a Wayfinding Plan should be a top priority and will help you "connect the dots" throughout your community.

The second a potential customer exits the highway into your community, they should have adequate signage that will help them find amenities, services and attractions. These signs should be decorative and should fit the communities "theme" instead of the standard aluminum municipal signage.

Kingman, Arizona is known as the "Heart of Route 66." The renowned cross-country route was made famous in the 1950s television show, the book *Grapes of Wrath*, and in countless songs (*Get Your Kicks on Route 66*). The city's new wayfinding program begins at the base of each freeway or highway exit and extends throughout the town. It not only plays up the theme, but also lets visitors know what the town has to offer and makes it easy for them to find the things that most interest them.

In the case of Kingman, four different types of signs were designed: entryway signage, banners along Route 66, directional signs (at each major intersection), and attractions signage (at the entry to each visitor attraction).

The journey that Lewis and Clark took was a difficult undertaking. Tourists, these days, are not looking for that type of challenge. Place your feet in the boots of those two historical trailblazers by identifying the quickest route from point A to point B and posting markers that show the way for those that follow.

Questions for Success:

Have you taken a close look at what visitors see as they enter your community?
Is your community a place you'd stop and shop if you were driving through?
Do local ordinances allow perpendicular signage?
Is your signage placed at a uniform height, similar in size, and decorative—fitting the overall

Rule 7

20/20 SIGNAGE EQUALS $$$

The rule of perpendicular signs

As you drive into a town for the first time, your vision is automatically directed forward through the windshield as you attempt to make sure you don't violate local traffic laws or cause an accident. You are also trying to find your way around town. You may be looking for a place to park or "checking the town out" to determine whether or not there's any reason to stop. This keeps the driver looking primarily forward, rather than from side-to-side.

Most visitors are, arguably, pretty good at obeying local traffic rules. However, few people have the peripheral vision required to both drive and see what a town has to offer. That is, of course, unless the town and local retailers know the importance of perpendicular signage.

Many shops in a downtown district simply place their signs above the door or have them painted on windows. More often than not, these signs are missed by potential customers totally unaware of what they have to offer or that they even exist. Even driving ten miles per hour through town will make it difficult to read this type of signage while watching for pedestrians in unfamiliar surroundings. Remember driver's education? Eyes forward!

Signs placed perpendicular to the building allow drivers to read them without turning their heads and can also be noticed from a further distance—a good thing.

To further improve readability, the letters must be tall enough to see at a distance. The general rule for lettering is one inch for every twelve feet of distance. Letters eight inches tall can be read from ninety-six feet away—about right for a downtown core area with visitors traveling fifteen to thirty-five miles per hour.

Pedestrians, too, will appreciate signs suspended over the sidewalk at a reasonable, consistent height. Have you ever had to crane your neck to figure out which store you wanted to enter because the signs were all displayed high atop the buildings? The Bavarian themed town of Leavenworth, Washington has done an excellent job of placing perpendicular signs that are easy to read by all visitors, whether they are in the car or on the sidewalk. In addition, they are also decorative and in keeping with the town's theme. Perpendicular signs of uniform height and similar size are less likely to obstruct one another, are more pleasing to look at, and are more effective in bringing in customers.

A common mistake made by many retailers is not telling the visitor what the store is actually selling. Visitors are not locals; therefore, store names are irrelevant and typically meaningless to them. Often, they are looking for a certain type of store, such as a restaurant, gallery, antique, or toy store. No one will know that Kelly's Laffin Crab sells windsocks and kites, but the shop probably gets a number of people interested in eating shellfish. Your perpendicular signs should advertise the type of store—the lure that will bring shoppers inside—while the window or door should be used for the actual name. Sell what you have, not who you are. This will greatly increase that coveted drop-in shopping traffic.

Imagine what would happen if the highway department placed road signs parallel to the road, instead of perpendicular—or if they used only one inch tall lettering, or a script type style. What works for them will also work for downtown storefronts. Perpendicular signage allows motorists to keep their eyes on the road AND see what you are selling.

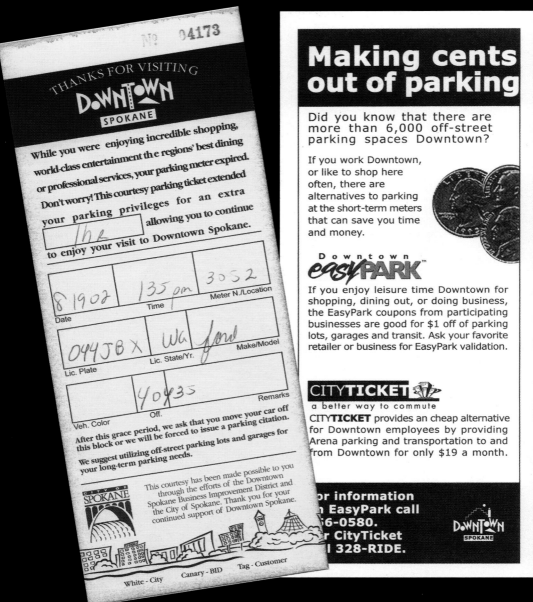

THANKS FOR VISITING

DOWNTOWN
SPOKANE

Nº 04173

While you were enjoying incredible shopping, world-class entertainment the regions' best dining or professional services, your parking meter expired. Don't worry! This courtesy parking ticket extended your parking privileges for an extra _ l hr _ allowing you to continue to enjoy your visit to Downtown Spokane.

Date	Time	Meter N./Location
8 19 02	135 pm	3052

Lic. Plate	Lic. State/Yr.	Make/Model
044JBX	WA	ford

Veh. Color	Off.	Remarks
	40935	

After this grace period, we ask that you move your car off this block or we will be forced to issue a parking citation. We suggest utilizing off-street parking lots and garages for your long-term parking needs.

This courtesy has been made possible to you through the efforts of the Downtown Spokane Business Improvement District and the City of Spokane. Thank you for your continued support of Downtown Spokane.

CITY OF SPOKANE

White - City   Canary - BID   Tag - Customer

Making cents out of parking

Did you know that there are more than 6,000 off-street parking spaces Downtown?

If you work Downtown, or like to shop here often, there are alternatives to parking at the short-term meters that can save you time and money.

Downtown easyPARK™

If you enjoy leisure time Downtown for shopping, dining out, or doing business, the EasyPark coupons from participating businesses are good for $1 off of parking lots, garages and transit. Ask your favorite retailer or business for EasyPark validation.

CITYTICKET
a better way to commute

CITYTICKET provides an cheap alternative for Downtown employees by providing Arena parking and transportation to and from Downtown for only $19 a month.

or information
n EasyPark call
56-0580.
r CityTicket
l 328-RIDE.

DOWNTOWN SPOKANE

QUESTIONS FOR SUCCESS:
- Do you have places for trucks and RVs to park?
- Do you have two hour (or shorter) parking limits that may be chasing customers away before they're done spending money in your community?
- Are your parking areas well signed, easy to find, and within a block of the downtown core area?
- Have you removed your parking restrictions after normal business hours?

Rule 8

PARKING IS NOT JUST FOR LOVERS

The parking limits rule

Imagine that you have just been lured into a community's shopping district. It's a delightful place, and you can't wait to begin your shopping spree. You pull into a parking space, feed the meter, and soon discover that the stores were every bit as wonderful as you thought they would be.

Going from shop to shop, your credit card stays nice and warm from its constant use, as you buy gifts for your friends and, of course, lots of things for yourself. Before you know it, you end up spending hundreds of dollars in this great little town. You are so excited, you can't wait to get back home to show friends what you bought and share your experience with them.

You are soon walking back to your car, arms full of packages, reveling in the thought of coming back with your friends so they too can discover this gem. As you get closer to your car, you notice a slip of paper tucked under the windshield wiper. Immediately your joy turns to irritation. You got a parking ticket for exceeding the two-hour limit. Aargh!

Shopping and dining in a pedestrian setting is the number one activity of visitors across the country, and the one activity that generates the most amount of revenue for the community—the primary benefit of tourism. So why do communities discourage shopping and dining by restricting the time customers can stay? Many communities chase visitors away before they are done spending, and they do it for the wrong reasons.

Towns typically post two-hour parking limits so local retail employees will be forced to park elsewhere. Employers are unable to teach their employees the relationship between parking and shopping, so they have the city enforce an arbitrary deadline. Inadvertently, towns punish their "customers" because they can't get local workers trained to park elsewhere. Of course, this also punishes local businesses who could generate more revenues if they would just give

their customers a chance to spend more time and money in their establishments.

Numerous studies have shown that shoppers—especially ones from out of town—take approximately four hours to satisfy their purchasing and dining needs. Visitors forced to keep watching the time usually leave before they complete their spending. Rarely will visitors go out, feed the meter, or move the car to another location, and then return to continue breaking out the plastic. They simply leave to spend their money elsewhere.

There are some communities that have discovered clever ways to help shoppers "shop 'til they drop." Spokane, Washington, a community that understands the importance of visitor spending, will put a "ticket" under the windshield wiper of cars in violation of the parking limit, but to the shoppers delight it states *"Thanks for visiting downtown Spokane. While you were enjoying incredible shopping, world-class entertainment, the region's best dining, or professional services, your parking meter expired. Don't worry! This courtesy parking ticket extended your parking privileges for an extra hour, allowing you to continue to enjoy your visit to Downtown Spokane."*

Another critical element is to provide locations for RV and truck parking. RV travel is increasing by double-digit numbers every year—and these folks have higher-than-average disposable incomes and room to store lots of "stuff." Don't put up signs that state "No RV or truck parking this block," without providing a solution: "RV and truck parking, next right."

Communities must recognize that the road to increased visitor spending and a vibrant downtown starts with plenty of tempting parking places with lots of time for spending. Successful communities will reap far more money from dollars spent in stores than from quarters spent in meters.

Rule 9

THE BELLMAN DOES MORE THAN JUST OPEN DOORS

The rule of frontline sales

You just finished a wonderful meal in a community that you know very little about. Rather than immediately getting in your car and heading towards your destination, you decide to walk off your meal by exploring the downtown area while doing some window-shopping. You enter one of the shops and begin talking with the employee behind the counter.

You ask, "How is it going?"
"Fine" the employee replies.
"Business good?"
"Not really."
"Lived here long?"
"All my life."
"Anything exciting to do in town?"
"No. This is Mayberry."

Does this seem like the sort of place where you would want to spend much time? Unlikely. In fact, this employee not only lost a sale in this store, but also probably discouraged you from doing anything else in the town—since there is nothing to do.

If, during the course of the above exchange, the employee engaged in any of the following behaviors—eye rolling, glaring, sighing impatiently, nursing a recent piercing, or ignoring you to discuss his or her love life with a fellow employee—you wouldn't even want to ask that person if there's anything to do. And your word-of-mouth endorsement of this community to the folks back home would be less than stellar.

Frontline employees are not just cashiers, stockers, wait staff, front desk personnel, or gas station attendants. They are also sales people for the community. In addition to making sales for the employer, they should sell events, attractions, and even the competition. Every dollar spent in the community will eventually become dollars in your pocket through increased tax revenues that will build parks, fix potholes, and encourage more visitors to your store for repeat spending experiences.

Frontline employees should be taught to ask three simple questions of their customers.

- Where are you from?
- How long will you be in town?
- Have you been to… (or what brings you to town)?

These three questions will usually spawn a short conversation in which your sales person can promote a local attraction that fits the customer's taste. The longer you can keep a customer in town, the more likely that person will spend some money there.

Huntsville, Texas, an historic town located about seventy miles north of Houston, has an attraction adoption program. When a visitor enters a shop and engages in a conversation with an employee, the employee encourages them to visit a particular site in the community. As visitors enter various stores, they'll find that each promotes a different attraction. Huntsville's merchants did a smart thing: each has "adopted" a local attraction, the employees are knowledgeable about the attraction, and they do everything they can to promote it.

This approach is much simpler than trying to train every front line employee about every attraction or site in town. Additionally, by adopting one attraction, the staff can really get to know it, and can better promote it as a "must see" thing to do while visiting the area.

Frontline employees are a major part of the sales effort. Make sure they know how important they are; when they open the doors to your store, they also open doors to the community.

EXAMPLE:

The town of Moses Lake, Washington found a handy location just off Interstate 90, and installed this "Information Station." The closeup (above) shows how they identified "must see" attractions including photos and teaser information. They are also identified on the map.

Ashland, Oregon knows the importance of providing visitor information. They not only have the 24 hour "directory" (lower right), but they also have a couple of stand-alone kiosks (lower left) which are staffed by volunteers. When the windows close for the evening, information is available in brochure holders (inside circle) so visitors can take information with them.

The primary objective of a visitor information center is to do exactly what its name implies: provide information to visitors. Typically, local chambers of commerce or convention and visitor bureaus are partially funded by lodging tax dollars, which visitors pay when they spend the night in the community. Hopefully, they are seeing some return on their investment in your community. Since a community never knows when a visitor will want information, the ideal VIC (Visitor Information Center) will stay open 365 days a year, 24 hours a day.

However, since most centers are staffed by volunteers that require occasional sleep, few are able to provide one-on-one contact with someone who may be passing through town any time of day or night.

This is where the kiosk—typically a small structure that stays open 365 days out of the year and never sleeps—comes in handy. Often made of wood, kiosks come in all sorts of sizes and shapes. They can be used to tell a story, or they can be used to promote events and attractions. Not only can they tell you where you are ("you are here!"), but they can also tell you where to go ("you can get there from here").

Location is critical for visitor information, and you should have kiosks at multiple locations. Each should be easily accessible from the highway and primary thoroughfares and should be identified with advance highway or directional signage. In the case of highways, communities should check with the state's transportation department for guidelines. This will also allow them to make sure that visitor information centers are given highway signage to direct visitors to the right location.

There are five keys to having a successful kiosk program in your community: first, each should be able to withstand all sorts of weather. They are the mail carriers of tourism. They stay out in the rain, snow, and sleet. They deliver messages that people need to have in order to enjoy your community, and their messages promote the area, making it worth a longer stay or another special trip.

Second, kiosks should fit the character of the town. Communities that have themes or a well-known event or attraction should build the kiosk with that in mind. The kiosk then becomes not only a source of information, but also a marketing tool.

Third, they should be maintained regularly with current information about events and activities. Have volunteers remove expired events.

Fourth, the kiosk should also include a "take one" weather-resistant display rack offering a printed "activities guide" that visitors can take with them. Local and area maps should be available and plentiful. And remember, the kiosk is primarily for visitors, so avoid making it a bulletin board for classified ads and local pancake feeds that have little or no interest to visitors.

Finally, you can never have enough visitor information sites. Convenience is critical. Not only should a kiosk be placed outside the doors to your visitor information center, but in other "stand alone" locations near your gateways and entrances to town. There should be one next to your public restrooms, in your shopping district, at major attractions and sites where they will cross-promote other sites. They should all have a similar look, user-friendly style, and should include photographs and brief text selling area attractions. Kiosks should be considered a sales tool—not just a location finder.

Kiosks should complement the volunteers that work at the visitor information centers, not replace them. They are not supposed to be substitutes for human contact. They are intended to let them have a good night's sleep. As the famous Motel 6 slogan says, "We'll leave the light on for you."

There are two types of retail stores in a community. There are "neighborhood retail" stores, which include hardware stores, professional services, taverns, pharmacies, grocery stores, and other shops geared primarily to local residents. "Visitor retail," on the other hand, includes gift shops, galleries, bookstores, antique dealers, clothing stores, collectibles, restaurants, espresso shops, souvenir shops, and arts and crafts stores, catering to both locals AND visitors. In some communities these are zoned separately but still convenient to one another.

If visitors want their shopping experience to be a real blessing and a truly religious experience, their best bet is to find a community that has visitor-oriented retail in a compact setting. This is what is referred to as critical mass.

You'll find that fast food restaurants and gas stations congregate on all four corners of an intersection because they all benefit from critical mass—lots of convenient choices in one spot. People will spend more money in a community if they don't have to drive from one shop to the next. It's typically not worth the hassle. It's just not convenient, and we are a nation where convenience is absolutely critical.

The town of Sisters, Oregon, (population 1,000) was a dying timber town in the '70s until Black Butte Ranch, a neighboring resort, began its development. Knowing how the resort's guests would want a pedestrian-oriented shopping district nearby, the resort offered Sisters building owners the money to help create facades on the dated buildings in the core three-block area along the highway. Over the years, the town took on a new appearance, and visitor-oriented retailers flocked to the newly designed shops. The neighborhood retail moved off the highway—they didn't need the highway exposure since local residents knew where they were.

The town of Chehalis, Washington, saw its many antique dealers congregate to a section of downtown, making the city the "antique capital of the Northwest." By locating thirty or forty stores together, they became convenient for visitors and locals alike. Would you make a special trip to a community to visit its outlet stores—knowing that the thirty stores were in different locations all over town? Would you feel differently if all of the stores were in a single location? Of course, you and millions of other outlet mall shoppers can attest to that.

By creating a critical mass of visitor-oriented establishments, towns can reap huge retail sales. As few as fifteen visitor-oriented retail shops with dining and treats within a couple of blocks can spur very strong retail sales and can totally revitalize a town. Communities that develop a pedestrian-friendly, visitor-oriented retail "village" end up succeeding and know that critical mass can truly be a blessing.

QUESTIONS FOR SUCCESS:
- What are the general perceptions of your community?
- Have you had a visitor assessment done?
- Have you taken a hard look at your "challenges" and how you might be able to turn those into "assets"?

The media have tremendous power in persuading people to do something or go somewhere. They provide movie reviews, restaurant ratings, and other commentary to help people enjoy themselves while spending their money wisely. More often than not, media reviews will have a positive impact on an establishment. However, if a community gets a bad review for a festival gone wrong, or if something negative takes place that is reported all over the country (or even in the region), its entire economy can be devastated.

It doesn't matter whether the information is correct or not. Once a negative comment is made, the story often takes on a life of its own, with little regard for its effect on the people who live in the area. However, a smart community with a bad review may find that it's not necessarily bad for business.

Battle Mountain, Nevada was designated by the Washington Post as "the armpit of America." A small, friendly community all of a sudden became the butt of late night TV humor as "Nowheresville." Similarly, Highway 50, connecting five communities in Nevada, was referred to as "the loneliest road in America" in a *LIFE* magazine interview with a person from the American Automobile Association. He went on to say that people would need a survival kit if they were to get stuck there.

Certainly these comments did nothing to enhance the reputation of Battle Mountain or the communities along Highway 50. They certainly dissuaded anyone from wanting to visit the areas.

Rural tourism officials in Nevada met with these communities and decided that they could do one of three things: they could be mad and write letters to the editor and even cancel their subscriptions; they could let it go and hope that no one read the articles, and wait for it to "go away;" or they could turn a negative into a positive. As you might imagine, they agreed to the latter.

Folks in Battle Mountain now promote the "Festival of the Pit." Instead of an old-fashioned egg toss they stage a deodorant toss as part of the festivities. The chamber has even purchased a billboard on I-80 encouraging motorists to make a "pit stop" in Battle Mountain. It also sent a blanket invitation to any community that has been considered an armpit: they can have a free booth at the festival if they'll just show up and staff it. Battle Mountain's stinky notoriety even landed them a sponsor for the event. Old Spice underwrites a portion of the activities. CNN and *USA Today* have covered the festival. And not only did *USA Today* run an article on the situation, they've offered to make bumper stickers saying, "Don't roll on by. Make Battle Mountain your next pit stop." You can't buy publicity like that. On top of all that, the community rallied together, and in just two weeks, hauled off more than forty tons of trash from around town. A major revitalization is now underway and Battle Mountain is seeing a resurgence in its community pride, and in its tourism industry.

The "Loneliest Road in America" was another challenge for Nevada's tourism commission. A "Survival Kit" was created, promoted, and available at retailers in every town along the route. It didn't take long before visitors from all over the country were exploring the loneliest road. It became a major tourist attraction. Along the way you'll find the "loneliest phone booth in America." Eureka, Nevada promotes itself as the "Friendliest town on the loneliest road in America." All this publicity brings tens of thousands of people annually to the area. It is a good example of Yogi Berra's maxim that "Nobody goes there anymore. It's too crowded."

Being stinky and lonely may not be attributes that you would want to put on a resume; however, a few choice hints to *USA Today* and CNN could turn that odor in the air into the smell of money rolling into your economy.

QUESTIONS FOR SUCCESS:

- What sets your community apart from everyone else?
- What do you have that makes you worth a special trip and that visitors can't get closer to home?
- What assets do you have that could become the "lure" to bring visitors to your community?
- Have you checked out the "competition" to make sure you're not marketing the same thing?

How would you like to spend some time attending the National Lentil Festival in the Palouse Region of Washington and Idaho? Or how about visiting Mike the Headless Chicken's annual events every third week in May in Fruita, Colorado?

They may not sound like the most exciting places to visit, yet tens of thousands of people flock to these communities every year to celebrate lentils and a chicken that supposedly lived for years without his head. People come from all over the world to feast on the largest pot of lentil soup or participate in a great game of Chicken Bingo (the numbers are chosen by where the chicken droppings fall on a numbered grid). What may seem rather insane to you means hundreds of thousands of dollars to the community with the idea. People, after all, like experiencing things that are unique. It makes these communities "worth the drive."

Coming up with an insane or uniqe idea does not mean that you have to be half-cocked in its development. It takes a great deal of consensus and planning in order to turn an idea into the "theme" that sets you apart and makes you worthy of a special trip. Your own brand of uniqueness may emerge in a variety of ways: architectural themes, event themes, or marketing themes.

Successful architectural theme towns include Leavenworth, Washington (Bavarian); Solvang, California (Danish); Winthrop, Washington (old west); and Sisters, Oregon (western). Successful event themes include Ashland, Oregon (Shakespeare Festival which runs nine months of the year); Branson, Missouri (music theater); and—well, Fruita, Colorado (Mike the Headless Chicken).

Another way to start the insane bandwagon is to look at the ideas of other communities. Don't copy them, but use them to inspire your own creative imagination. Let's say you start with Mike the chicken. We can agree that headless chickens are out—been there,

done that. But maybe your community is the rubber chicken capital of the world…or it is rumored to have been the inspiration for The Headless Horseman…or there was that flying pig incident back in the 1920s.

Americans may find comfort in the familiarity of a Wal-Mart in every town and a McDonald's on every corner, but they will seek out that which is truly unique. Sometimes it is as close as the nearest garage. It just so happens that a gentleman in St. Maries, Idaho, (pronounced Saint Mary's) has collected every model Corvette ever manufactured, and has every Corvette Indy pace car in his collection. While St. Maries has a timber heritage, can you imagine the pull if the whole town adopted a Corvette theme, with every store adopting a model year and, if there's room, putting one of the collection inside the store or just outside? Can you imagine the number of Corvette clubs, rallies, and classic car events that would gravitate to scenic St. Maries? Once there, visitors could then learn more about St. Maries, including its timber heritage. The Corvette theme would be a powerful magnet.

A car museum is rather ordinary. Having the whole town adopt the theme, with Corvettes in nearly every shop, would make St. Maries extraordinary.

In order to be successful in tourism, you must set yourself apart from everyone else. If you offer the same thing a visitor can get closer to home, then why should they make a special trip to see you? There really is no such thing as an insane idea. One man's headless chicken is another community's goose that laid the golden egg.

QUESTIONS FOR SUCCESS:

- What do you have that makes you better than competing communities closer to the population centers you are trying to attract?
- Have you searched for third-party endorsements in books, magazine articles, and other sources?

Standing ovations typically take place in the theater, at a concert, or at an awards banquet. They are reserved for those people who have completed an excellent performance. A standing ovation is a spontaneous outpouring of appreciation for people who have truly done something outstanding in their craft. They are reserved only for the best.

Your community should strive to get a standing ovation from every person that visits. After all, the attractions, events, or amenities you provide should exceed all others in quality. That makes you worth a special trip. Why promote something that is good when you can attract people by being great? By being the best, people will go out of their way to see you over a similar experience closer to home. People have lots of choices when they travel. They have plenty of options for activities and attractions. However, the chances are that you are not the only one that provides a certain activity. You are competing with thousands of other communities across the country to capture the visitor dollar.

There are 425 counties in the eleven western states of the U.S. Not surprisingly, every one of them promotes outdoor recreation as a primary activity—even the urban areas. Hundreds of counties and thousands of communities in these states promote hiking, biking, horseback riding, surfing, snowmobiling, skiing, bird watching, or sightseeing. Many proclaim "we have it all." They continuously tell people that they have "hundreds of miles of hiking and biking trails." But if someone can find those same activities closer to home, why should they make a special trip to a community located farther away?

Case in point: Okanogan County is located in north central Washington, just below the Canadian border. Spectacularly beautiful with hundreds of miles of trails and "year-round recreation," it still wasn't attracting visitors from the lucrative Seattle market. Why? The thirteen counties closer to the metropolitan area were promoting the same thing, so why drive an extra two hours to visit Okanogan County?

So, the folks in "Okanogan Country" scoured the guidebooks for quotes from people who have actually experienced the recreational activities there and began running ads using quotes they found: *"Rocky Mountain powder in the Northwest? Go ahead, pinch yourself, you're in the Methow Valley." "Perhaps the best cross-country skiing on the continent." "Without a doubt, the best mountain biking in the lower 48." "A must visit destination for anyone, of any age, who owns or wants to snowmobile."* Quotes like these now make Okanogan Country worth the extra drive.

People travel from around the world to ski at Whistler Resort in British Columbia. Why? Because it's been awarded the distinction of being the "Best ski resort in North America" for ten years running.

Simply self-proclaiming that you're "the best" won't cut it. You need that third-party endorsement. Cozumel, Mexico, located in the Caribbean with hundreds of other legendary islands, was competing for a share of the lucrative dive market, but had a hard time distinguishing itself from Aruba, Jamaica, the Virgin Islands, Barbados, and countless other islands. That was until Cozumel was labeled as the "drift diving capital of the world" by *Skin Diver Magazine*. This is now the thrust of Cozumel's marketing effort to the dive community. By being the best, and being recognized by credible sources as such, Cozumel has seen great success.

Communities should develop attractions that will make them the absolute best. Your goal is to get every visitor to stop their car on the way out of town, get out, turn towards the town, and begin to applaud because your performance was so extraordinary.

QUESTIONS FOR SUCCESS:

- What are the biggest draws to your community?
- Do you have the supporting businesses necessary to make those activities successful?
- Do you promote the supporting businesses or just the activity?
- Do you have a tourism-business attraction and retention program?
- Are you working with supporting businesses to promote your attractions and activities?

Can you imagine buying a ticket to a movie where one person did everything? They were the star, the director, the producer, the grip, the casting agent, and even the best boy. It doesn't happen. There's a good reason why so many people work on a successful production. It's because no matter how big a star, no matter how good a job they do in marketing the show, the actor is nothing without a supporting cast. Filmmaking really is a team effort.

In successful tourism, there is never only one business holding up the entire industry. Not even Disneyland can do it alone. It needs airports, rental car companies, hotels, restaurants, and even other attractions that will keep people in the area longer.

Communities can develop an entire marketing campaign for their greatest attraction, but without supporting businesses, the attraction will never reach its full potential. Thirty years ago, Whistler Resort in British Columbia was just another rural community with about 750 residents and a dream. Whistler started as a seasonal ski destination, and most of the town's retail businesses couldn't survive the remaining seven months of each year. Then in the early 1980s, the development of the renowned Whistler Village began to take shape as a backdrop to the mountain attraction. Whistler Village is now home to nearly 200 retail shops, 85 restaurants, and 3,500 first-class accommodations. Additionally, there are mountain bike rentals, river rafting guides, two golf courses, and a host of other "supporting businesses." Even though Whistler is rated as the "Best Ski Resort in North America," it now does more business in the summer than in the winter months. Oh, the power of supporting businesses.

Not every community will have a mountain in their backyard, but most have attractions that are unique to the area. If hiking and biking trails are your claim to fame, seek out retail businesses such as bike rental, sales, and repair shops; tour guides; and supply stores. Sprinkle in a few restaurants and hotels that have lockers for bikes and gear, and you've got the makings of your supporting cast.

How do you find a supporting cast? The first rule of any business recruitment program is to ask your primary attraction, "What are the businesses that would help you be successful in bringing in more visitors or getting them to stay longer?" They will provide a list of suppliers as well as amenities and other attractions that will keep people spending money in the area for days, if not weeks. Primary attractions know the advantages of having their suppliers close by and a range of diverse activities. They even appreciate competitors, knowing that the presence of one supports the other.

Communities also want to make sure that the supporting cast can be successful all year round. After all, being the best ski destination is only a four-month run. Whistler pioneers wanted the area to become more than just a winter resort, so their businesses could succeed. That is why you'll find the lifts open for mountain bikers and hikers during the "off season."

Whistler may continue to receive accolades as the number one ski destination in North America, but the supporting businesses are reaping the rewards of being profitable all year long.

Questions for Success:

- Do you tell stories in your museums, or simply show artifacts?
- How long does the average visitor spend in your museum(s)?
- Are your stories interesting enough to capture the visitor and entice them to return?
- Are the displays unique and captivating?
- Have you included interesting stories about local buildings or sites as part of your program?

The rancher's cattle were disappearing at alarming rates. A look at the dusty terrain did not uncover any human footprints, so they must not have been rustled. But carcasses weren't found either, ruling out wild animals. And since the fields were fenced, the Nevada rancher was quite sure the cattle didn't just wander off.

After months of agonizing losses, the rancher sent out a couple of farm hands to stake out the fields. They bedded down on a hilltop, and at dawn one morning, they heard loud whooping and hollering and the sounds of bellowing cattle in the valley down below. They scrambled out of their sleeping bags and ran down the hill as fast as they could to where the cattle were gathered. With guns loaded and cocked, they stopped, dead in their tracks, gaping in amazement…

Storytelling has been a form of entertainment since the Stone Age. It began with stories around the campfire and etchings on the cave wall and has progressed to bedtime stories and midnight readings of Harry Potter. Storytelling, like opposable thumbs, is a characteristic that distinguishes humans from all other animals. Stories entertain, teach, establish moral precedents, and recall our genealogy. They can do just about anything and always bring people together—including bringing visitors into a community.

Cultural tourism is the fastest growing segment in the tourism industry. It takes visitors on a journey of discovery, beyond the gift shops and amusements and into the community's soul—its history, environment, and the arts.

Museums are a mainstay of cultural tourism. They will often display items from the town and showcase some of the unusual characters that lived there. But many museums fail because they simply show artifacts rather than tell stories. They have collections of old bottles, typewriters, furniture, industry equipment, and all sorts of memorabilia that have meaning but no context. What makes a museum successful is its ability to tell stories, either oral or written. An artifact without a story is just something to look at. But a story brings it alive. It makes it real and memorable. And it keeps visitors longer, which translates to more spending.

Museums that tell great stories will captivate visitors for hours, and they'll develop a bond with the community. Best of all, they'll tell other people, who more than likely will have to see it, read it, or hear it for themselves.

And now, for the rest of the story:
…they stopped, dead in their tracks, gaping in amazement as they came face to face with the old crook, Crazy Tex Hazlewood, rustling the rancher's cattle while wearing the novel shoes you see shown on the opposite page.

Want to see, read, and hear some more great stories? Visit the Northeastern Nevada Museum in Elko. But beware; you'll be there for hours.

QUESTIONS FOR SUCCESS:
- Have you taken a look at your activities and their drawing power?
- Have you determined who your major market is?
- Do you have the activities that make visiting your community worth the drive?
- Have you explored how you use the Four Times Rule?

Rule 17

THE SHORTEST DISTANCE BETWEEN TWO POINTS IS A GOOD TIME

The Four-Times rule

If you live in a rural area and need to make periodic trips to the big city, do you develop a mental list and run a number of errands while you are there? Sure. You are making it "worth the drive" by getting more done and saving precious time. You certainly don't want to spend more time in the car than you do in the shops.

When it comes to tourism, people determine their trips the same way. People will visit your community if you have activities that interest them, and that will keep them busy four times longer than it took to get them there. So if you expect a visitor to drive fifteen minutes to see you, you'll need to have at least an hour's worth of activities in order to make it worth the drive. This is referred to as the Four Times Rule.

If your community is located an hour from the major population area from which you are trying to attract, you need to have four hour's worth of activities that cater to that visitor.

Planners and builders often utilize this rule when making their decisions on where to locate facilities. For example, when a movie theater decides on a location, knowing that most movies are about two hours long, they look at the population within a twenty- to thirty-minute radius. Few people will travel more than twenty minutes just to see a movie, unless it's, once again, combined with other activities like shopping or dining.

The Four Times Rule will determine your major market area. The more you have to offer and the more powerful your draw, the further people will travel to see you. Look at Branson, Missouri with its thirty music theaters—it's a national draw.

The Four Times Rule also determines whether or not you can become an overnight destination. To lure overnight visitors to your primary attractions, you need to have at least eight hours of activities that will

cater to the visitor. Your community must also have the other amenities that go with overnight stays: lodging, dining, entertainment, and supporting businesses.

The ultimate goal of a community with a focus on tourism is to become worthy of a multi-day visit—and not just seasonally, but on a year-round basis. After all, overnight visitors spend three times that of day visitors. The most successful areas that create multiple night visits are called destinations. These communities are worth a "special trip." You may have heard of a few of these: Orlando, Branson, Hawaii, Disneyland, and Yellowstone National Park.

Let's say you really need a break; highly unlikely, but let's just pretend. Would you buy (at regular prices) a ticket to Hawaii, leave Saturday morning, get there late Saturday, then come back Sunday afternoon in time for work Monday morning? Chances are, you'd probably call in sick or take some additional vacation days—to make it worth the trip. This is why the average stay in remote locations, like Hawaii, is typically a week or longer.

The same rationale works for smaller communities as well. What makes you worth the drive? Do you have enough to offer to become a destination community?

Take a look at your "staying power," and it will tell you who your market is.

Traveling in cars and planes used to be fun and exciting, but lately it has become much more time consuming and uncomfortable. Communities need to create an environment that people will look forward to—where the pleasure of community activities and attractions outweighs the discomfort of travel. Only then will people remember that the quality of the visit outweighed the length of time it took to get there.

QUESTIONS FOR SUCCESS:

- Do your tourism efforts include both product development and marketing?
- Is there a good balance between the two?
- Are you under so much pressure to make something happen "now" that most of the funds are spent on marketing, even though you know product development is sorely needed?

Cash flow is the lifeblood of the economy. The goal of every business is to have enough cash coming in so that you can pay the bills and improve what you have to offer. As long as more money is coming into the business than is going out, people are happy. The benefit of tourism is that it is an "import industry." Visitors come into town, spend money, then go home—importing cash into the local economy. Successful communities import more cash than they export (when residents spend money elsewhere that they've earned locally).

A goal of just about every community is to effectively promote their attractions and events, which will assist in keeping their businesses in positive cash flow. The more money that goes into effective promotion, the more local businesses will reap as a result of visitor spending. The more money a business makes, the greater the tax collections that go back to the community. The more money the community collects, the more money that is available with which to promote. Thus, the cycle continues, always improving the business climate and opening up opportunities for new and growing businesses.

While the marketing effort is important, it should not be the only priority. Many communities make this mistake, when they should be investing in upgrading or adding to their product. If a business puts all of its money in advertising and little or nothing into inventory or product development, the business will ultimately fail. Quite often, travelers will visit a community as a result of the marketing effort and go home disappointed, never to visit again. For others, when it comes time to plan the next trip, they will cross you off the list as a "been there, done that" community. Others won't be convinced that you have enough to offer to make a special trip in

the first place, and others will simply know better. The point is that every single community should make product development the top priority. Things to do. Activities. Attractions. Amenities. ALWAYS invest and budget in product development FIRST, then as the product gets developed, tip the scales more towards marketing. A smart community will spend 90 percent of its available tourism budget on product development, and as the product gets better and better, the scales are gradually tipped to perhaps 50 percent product development and 50 percent marketing.

While every community is different, the scales should never be tipped to more than about 70 percent for marketing. Product development never ends—it's an ongoing process and should ALWAYS be the priority. After all, your product is really why people visit you. Keep adding to it and making it better, and you'll get more repeat business, have a longer season, and a strong "brand" that will require less effort to market.

Product development is not just for community events and attractions that draw visitors. It includes signage, wayfinding, visitor information kiosks, public restrooms, theme development, beautification, supporting businesses, etc. Communities must also make sure that they talk to their businesses and find out what infrastructure should be upgraded or developed to help them further enhance their product so that people keep coming back. This is part of a "business retention program." Without a strong business retention program that supports the businesses and their needs, a tourism program will never succeed.

The result will be a continued cash flow that will keep both the businesses and community happy.

QUESTIONS FOR SUCCESS:

- Are you selling activities or places?
- Does the text in your marketing materials evoke emotion?
- Are you simply listing activities or are you taking the time to tell visitors WHY they should take part in those activities?

River rafting in Okanogan Country, Washington

SELL THE RAPIDS, NOT THE RIVER

The rule of selling the experience

One of the most spectacular places to river raft in the Northwest is along the Skykomish River, near the little town of Index, Washington. A spot along the run is called Boulder Drop, and is rated—on a scale of one to five—a four according to many guidebooks. A five rating is the most treacherous. What makes it remarkable is the clear blue water that allows you to see to the bottom of the river, followed by a sudden rush of frothing white water rushing around huge boulders and dropping off into ten-foot waterfalls, which you attempt to navigate around and through. The ice cold water slaps you in the face as you try to navigate the raft toward the next spot of calm water without capsizing and leaving stranded rafters floating down the river or hanging onto the huge boulders.

As you tighten your grip on the oar while attempting to see through the water in your eyes and hear the laughter and screams of your friends (mainly screams), all thoughts leave your mind. You're in the moment, living only for that rush of adrenaline.

The next time you think about Index, you will probably remember Boulder Drop and the excitement and the cool mist on your face; you won't care whether the town was named Index or Thumb or Ringfinger.

All too often, communities get stuck promoting the place and not the activities. Visitors are far more interested in the things to do than in the location. People will travel farther to feel the rush of 40-degree water splashing over them than to visit a quaintly named town that sounds a lot like quaint towns closer to home.

County marketing groups are notorious for promoting the county as a destination. Have you ever gone anywhere because it was a county? Would you prefer to visit the world-renowned Napa Valley or Napa County? Napa County sounds like a governmental entity, while Napa Valley sounds like a beautiful place to see and visit. The Napa Valley is widely known as Wine Country, which truly gets to the heart of the experience, and why it's known worldwide.

How do you make the experience tangible for someone who is still sitting at home in his or her armchair? One of the least expensive channels is the Internet. Brief, eloquent descriptions of your surroundings, accompanied by professionally shot photographs and third-party reviews, will lead visitors to the water and make them grab the nearest raft. As high-speed connections become the norm, action-packed short movie clips (it only takes a few seconds) delivered over the Internet can bring activities to life and make visitors "want to go there."

One of the most popular forms of promotion is the development of an "Activities Guide" rather than a standard brochure. This is a multi-page booklet or brochure that dedicates at least one page to each of your major activities or attractions. Too many brochures provide only lists of things to see and do, when photos and descriptions "selling the experience" would be a more effective lure. The more you have to offer, the longer people will stay, and the more likely they will return. Even using the simple words "Activities Guide" tells a potential customer that you have things to do. The word "brochure" says nothing. Would you be more likely to "call for your free brochure" or "call for your free Activities Guide to the Northwest's best river rafting"? We all want things to do, not just things to see.

Effective tourism marketing revolves around two words: Evoke Emotion. The thrill of the roller coaster; the relaxing, serene feeling of sitting on a quiet beach at sunset; or screaming at the top of your lungs as your raft spins sideways and drops down over the waterfall. Once you can effectively "sell the experience," people will flock to your location.

QUESTIONS FOR SUCCESS:
- What do you have that clearly sets you apart and that you can build your brand around?
- Are your local organizations on the same page in terms of developing your brand?
- Do your events follow the marketing "theme" or "image" you are trying to build?

Rule 20

MAKE IT EASY TO TELL YOUR COWS FROM MY COWS

The rule of branding

The Romans used brands as symbols to identify their professions. A row of hams depicted the butcher's trade, a cow symbolized a dairyman, and a boot reflected a cobbler. The markings represented crafts rather than specific craftsmen. Soon after, Romans began using their brands to advertise themselves, while the Egyptians seared insignias into livestock to identify their stray or stolen animals. This latter custom was passed on to ranchers and became the symbol of ownership in a business where ownership was everything. Branding became such a big part of a rancher's life, that they used to say that a good cowboy could recognize and understand the Constitution of the United States if it were only written with a branding iron on the side of a cow.

Branding your community is the process of setting yourself apart from everyone else. In tourism, communities want the visitor to subconsciously associate the brand with something they will easily recognize and remember. As soon as they see your name, or what it is you are known for, they will remember you as a place they'd like to visit.

The association may involve any or all of the senses. When you hear the word "Disneyland" you may picture mouse ears, the Matterhorn, and Goofy and automatically associate it with fun, fantasy, and families. You really don't think of Anaheim, where Disneyland is located. Disneyland is the "brand" and and the activity associated with the city.

People familiar with the garlic festival in Gilroy, California, may have an olfactory or gastronomical sensation upon hearing about that event. And everyone knows that "Virginia is for lovers," according to a long and successful campaign.

Branding is much more than slogans and logos. It is not an easy strategy for a community to undertake. In the first place, it requires the varied disciplines of business (product development), marketing,

communications, and graphic design. Second, it requires complete buy-in from the community, in order to send a consistent message in all marketing programs. Third, it takes time. Communities that are in a rush to get their brand known will inevitably fail as a result of poor planning and inadequate feedback. Budweiser didn't become the "King of Beers" overnight.

Building a brand requires a concerted public relations effort. Public relations is used to build the brand, while advertising maintains your position once you're on top. The branding process includes repositioning (for communities turning themselves around), image (defining who you are), market definition (defining who you hope to attract), and finding your niche (defining the unique feature that will attract visitors). Then you promote it like crazy.

Tourism is not the first industry to try to brand itself for market share. Companies have been doing it for years, and communities are finally getting the idea. If you want customers to choose your community when there are dozens of communities closer to home, you'll need to let them to know the difference between your cows and the cows next door.

QUESTIONS FOR SUCCESS:
- Have you budgeted for the development of a photo library?
- Do you have a photo library?
- Does your photo library include activities more than scenic vistas?
- Do your photos have "wow!" appeal?
- Have you looked at other ads, brochures and/or websites to see what a difference photography can make in closing the sale?

Nothing sells tourism as well as photography. The use of outstanding photography should truly sell the experience. The picture of a resort is nice, but what makes the sale is the photo of the guest playing tennis or lying by the pool. People are looking for experiences, things to do—activities. Don't show the river—show the kayakers. Don't show the water slides, show the fun. Your photos should evoke emotion—they should make a potential customer say "Wow. I want to go there," or "That looks like fun!"

Brochures and advertisements are the most expensive parts of any tourism strategy. You want to provide enough information to guide people to the next step: making plans and making reservations. Too much text and you'll lose your audience. Photographs are a way to tease people—to pull them into your ad, article, or Activities Guide. They are a way to say, "This could be you climbing or hiking or getting that relaxing massage."

Every community should develop a professional photo library with between sixty and one hundred photographs. They should showcase every season, and at least 75 percent of them should feature people enjoying activities. While scenic vistas may create ambiance, in reality, they capture the visitor for only a few minutes. Your goal is to entice people to come and spend money in the community—not stop for a minute, look, and then leave.

The best way to begin your search for photos is to go to a bookstore and look at the numerous pictorial travel books that feature your area. You will generally see books that are filled with stunning photography. Look at the credits and make contact with the photographer(s) to ask if you can use some of their photos to promote the area.

Another way to seek out photos is to identify the professional photographers in your region and tell them that you are looking to promote the area with highlighted events and activity photos. It will be easy to distinguish between those that take wedding and graduation pictures and those that take action shots.

Costs can vary, but expect to pay for quality work. Think of this as an investment. Every person that looks at photos of your community could be spending some money as a result of the picture you choose.

Expect to negotiate with the photographer. This is their work, and they take great pride in it. They not only want to make sure they are compensated fairly, but also that the photos are presented correctly. Most photographers will retain the rights and limit your use. You should expect to professionally digitize the photos in a large, high-resolution format. Anything else will diminish their quality.

Many communities make a limited number of high-resolution photos available on their websites for use by the media. Working on deadline, a publisher may discover a hole that needs filling after regular working hours. You can be a hero to the editor and improve the odds that a story about your community will be seen and read by offering 24-hour access to online photos. Some websites require registration before downloading photos to discourage inappropriate distribution of these professional images.

Some communities will seek to have photos taken by amateurs. Some even hold periodic photo contests. Though these photos can be kept in the library and displayed at community events, they rarely meet the professional standards required for marketing materials. Remember, these photos will be used to entice people to come and stay in your community. They must have "wow" appeal.

Photos are not only worth a thousand words; if they get people to stay for multiple days, your photos will be worth a thousand nights. Room nights, that is.

QUESTIONS FOR SUCCESS:

- What was it that convinced you to book your last vacation trip?
- Are your marketing materials good enough to close the sale?
- How do your materials stack up?
- Is the top 3" of your brochure good enough to capture the attention of a potential customer?
- Do your brochures sell activities–things to do?

Newspapers, brochures, magazines, special events, direct mail, trade shows, the Internet, television, radio, transit advertising, billboards, dioramas—these are just a few of the tools and outlets that companies use to get people to buy their products. People are bombarded hundreds of times every day with someone trying to sell them something. Watching television for just one hour will expose you to nearly fifty commercials. Looking at a magazine or newspaper may expose you to twice that amount. The bottom line? Your marketing materials MUST be good enough the close the sale. Each piece may be your last opportunity to convince a potential visitor to pick you over the next destination or event.

An excellent advertising or PR program can get potential visitors to call for your "free Activities Guide" or get them to log on to your website, but both better be good enough the close the sale. Otherwise, your marketing dollars are largely wasted.

There is an old saying that "I know that half my advertising dollars are wasted. The problem is I don't know which half." It's not really very funny if you're the one spending the money. Most communities waste more than 85 percent of their marketing dollars because they fail to understand how to market effectively. That's right, 85 percent. Pick up a magazine or the travel section of the Sunday paper. Look through the travel ads. Which ones are good enough to get you to make a call or log on to a website? Then, when you get the brochure or look at the website, which places effectively convince you to go there?

Every community promotion, regardless of the medium, should do two primary things: First, it must create a positive image of your community. People want to visit places that are reputable—places that seem like a "nice place to go." Visitors want to see and experience events and attractions that are highly regarded, either by word of mouth or by objective third parties. It's not necessary to use a lot of text. Short quotes from recognizable people will go a long way toward bringing customers to you.

Second, there must be a call to action. This spells out the next step and often provides an incentive: "Call for our free Activities Guide to the best snowmobiling in the Lower 48," or "Take a virtual tour at www.ourtown.com." It must take the reader to the next step: either getting them to call for more information, log on to the website, or make those plans and reservations.

The top two to three inches of your brochure, Activities Guide, or ad must grab the reader's eye, while the bottom should have your potential customer grabbing for the phone or a pencil in order to write down the number or website address.

Tens of thousands of communities spend more than $2 billion each year (in the U.S. alone) trying to get visitors to their community. That's a lot of marketing! The competition for the tourist dollar is tremendous—and growing as more and more communities try to diversify towards tourism.

In the race to win people's vote as the place to spend their precious time off (and spend their hard-earned travel money), second place doesn't count. You are either chosen or not. Winning marketing programs create winning communities.

Rule 23

BRAGGING IS MORE EFFECTIVE WHEN SOMEONE ELSE DOES IT FOR YOU

The rule of public relations

Oyez, Oyez (roughly translated as "hark" or "listen") became a familiar call in town squares, markets, and public meeting places all over Britain in the 1700s. Town criers used those words to summon the townspeople to gather and listen to news of plague, victories in far-off lands, royal births, and deaths by execution.

Criers were usually people of some standing in the community, as they had to be able to read and write the proclamations. The crier would read a proclamation or inform the public of matters of importance. They were considered the first "talking newspaper," but in reality they were the mouthpieces that promoted the king's actions and programs. In modern times, we call them public relations people, but their duties are still the same: to promote the client from a third party's viewpoint, and to spread the word.

Public relations is a vital and very important, but often overlooked, complement to advertising. Studies have shown that 10 percent of vacationers choose their trips as a result of ads they see, 40 percent as a result of an article they have read, and 50 percent because of word-of-mouth recommendations made by friends or family.

Together, advertising and public relations can easily account for more than half your visitor spending, and it's important to have a balance between them.

With advertising, you pay for the privilege of seeing your message run in a guaranteed position, exactly as you wrote it. With public relations, the route is less direct. You "suggest" a good story and hope it will be picked up by the news media, trade publications, and websites. The cost is always lower, but you have less control over the final message. You pay for advertising, you pray for good PR.

Given the relative lack of control, why is public

relations so successful? Credibility. A magazine may publish an article that you have provided, verbatim, but to the reader there is an appearance of objectivity. Public relations generates a third party endorsement, while in advertising you're tooting your own horn.

Moreover, articles are three times more likely to be read than paid ads. People subscribe to the local paper and magazines for the articles, not the ads.

Some people think "PR" means sending out a few press releases. A good public relations program goes much, much further, establishing relationships with editors and sometimes creating stories—and attention—where none existed beforehand.

Paying a professional public relations firm to place articles in targeted outlets should be a priority and is always cost effective. Print, radio, and television ads can cost an enormous amount and must appear regularly in order to be effective. In comparison, public relations offers a greater return on investment. Some studies have shown that $3 of publicity (referred to as "earned media") is attained for every $1 spent on a public relations campaign.

Bragging about your community is fine, as long as you let others do it. Some communities may decide that it is time to bring back the town crier, who can act as an ambassador, deployed to draw attention to special events and attractions in your area.

Oyez, oyez, oyez.

Back in the 1960s, the phone company developed a marketing campaign that encouraged people to use their product more. "Let your fingers do the walking" became synonymous with picking up the yellow pages and finding a place to do business with over the phone. People still use their fingers to do their walking, but they are more likely to be found on a keyboard than on a dial pad.

Just as the Internet has changed the way people shop, it also has changed the way people plan and book their vacations. They simply type in the area they want to visit, or the activity they want to experience, and they'll instantly have hundreds of listings in front of them.

So how can your area compete on the super highway? Assuming that your community already has something of interest for the tourist, there are hundreds of ways to make your site stand out. Here are a few:

• Make the site informational but not wordy. Research has shown that users are more likely to read web content that is concise and factual.

• The site should answer any questions that the visitor may have. They want to know, "What is there to do? How do I get around? Where do I stay? Are there any package deals? Are there special activities for kids, seniors? What's going on this month?"

• Think about organizing your site by the type of activities available, from a menu that asks, "What do you want to do?" Also include testimonials from satisfied visitors—those third-party endorsements.

• Make your Activities Guide and other literature available for download as PDF files.

• To ensure that your site is seen by the greatest number of visitors, establish mutual links with other tourism-oriented websites and register with the most popular search engines.

• Find a qualified, professional web designer. Go for experienced rather than just local. With the Internet, every web designer is at the tip of your fingers. And, make sure you budget properly. A good website is meant to show your best qualities. Don't use inexpensive design templates. A minimum budget for a quality site will be at least $20,000, and $45,000 is not too much to spend.

• Use lots of photography, especially activity shots. Potential tourists want to get as close to visiting your community as they can without actually setting foot on your sidewalks. Photos will draw people in. The text will close the sale. A word of caution, however: graphics are the number-one cause of slow download times.

• Photos should be optimized for quicker downloading. If you want to display a lot of photos on one page, use thumbnail images that users can click if they want to see a larger size. Carefully screen photos and use only those that contribute to the story.

Internet users want results, and they want them now. Travelers use their computers to book flights and reserve rooms. If your site doesn't offer that e-commerce connection, make sure it provides links to those sites that do. Offer an e-mail link to answer any questions. To stay in front of customers, invite them to sign up for an e-newsletter with upcoming events and special savings.

The Internet has become a remarkable tool for people who want to plan their vacations from the comfort of their home. Nimble fingers and a ready mouse pad are all it takes. It has also become a marketing tool for communities that will encourage people to get out of their homes and see what is great about this country. The Internet may be a great place to let your fingers do the walking, but a great site will get people out to let their feet do the walking through your community.

QUESTIONS FOR SUCCESS:
- Are you using "TOMA" in your marketing efforts?
- When you think of a fast-food restaurant, what's the first name that pops into your mind? Why?
- When someone wants to experience what you have to offer (let's say mountain biking) are you the first place that comes to mind?

Rule 25

REPETITION GETS RESULTS, REPETITION GETS RESULTS

The rule of frequency

We all have sayings that we live by—"don't forget to wear clean underwear," or "don't talk with your mouth full." Our mothers put them in our heads, and even though we ignored them when we were young, we remember them now and pass them on to our children. We remember them not because they were so wise, but because our mothers kept repeating them to us over and over and over again until they sunk in.

In tourism, repetition is often the key to getting people to visit your community. How many times have you heard the announcer approach the most valuable player after the Super Bowl and ask, "Where are you going after the game?" The player then responds, "I'm going to Disneyland!" People have been talking about and making fun of that ad for years. Yet it works. People remember it, and at one time in their lives have probably gone to Disneyland.

Frequency creates "Top of Mind Awareness" (TOMA). When people think, "Gee, it would be good to get away for a few days," you want your community to be the one that comes to mind. If it's on their minds, it's either because they have been there before, or because they have heard about it enough times for it to register. In the newspaper industry, they sell TOMA packages for this very purpose. When people make decisions to go to a new place, it is more than likely that they have seen or heard about it numerous times.

Ads typically need to be seen five times before they are remembered. You are far better off running an ad in a single magazine five times (or more) than you are running the same ad once in five different publications. At least the readers of the single magazine will remember you; your ad will barely register a blip on the radar of readers with only one exposure.

In order to be successful, your ads and exposure must be frequent. Some of the most effective ads on television would be considered terrible by most

standards, but because they are played so often, you remember them. And in tourism, that is the name of the game: be remembered.

Tied to frequency is consistency. While you may see the same photo, the same slogan, the same ad promoting your community time and time again, the customer doesn't see it as often as you do. If there is too much variation between messages, it's the same as running a different ad for a different community each time. And there goes the "five times rule." Rather than remembering five distinct messages, each seen only once, the customer will remember none of them. You can easily use the same slogan or concept for two or three years, depending on the campaign.

Chances are, when people see or hear your ad, they may not be planning a trip or even a quick getaway. But when they do sit down and think about where they would like to go, you want their mind to travel to your ad. Say it once, say it twice, then say it again and again. Frequency sells. Repetition gets results. Repetition gets results.

The Authors

Roger Brooks is the President of Destination Development, Inc., which specializes in tourism and resort development and marketing with offices in Olympia, Washington and Salt Lake City, Utah. Over the past twenty plus years, Roger has assisted more than 160 communities, dozens of counties and states, and privately developed destination resorts in their efforts to further develop their client base and the tourism industry. Additionally, he has recruited more than three billion dollars of private investment to destination resorts and communities, and has amassed an outstanding record of success. His tell-it-like-it-is, bottom line approach, and tremendous enthusiasm for the industry has empowered organizations around the world in their tourism efforts, and has made Roger one of the most sought after

Maury Forman, Ph.D., is the Director of Education and Training for the Washington State Department of Community, Trade and Economic Development. He was the winner of the American Economic Development Council's Preston Award in 1998 for outstanding contributions in educational advancement, the U.S. Small Business Administration's 1998 Vision 2000 Award, and the ROI Research Institute Award for Innovation in Adult Education. He is a popular speaker across the country and is known as an educator and humorist. Dr. Forman is the author and editor of numerous books on economic development, including *Race to Recruit, Learning to Lead, Washington Entrepreneurs Guide, Community Wisdom, How to Create Jobs Now and Beyond 2000, and Journey to Jobs*

The Organizations

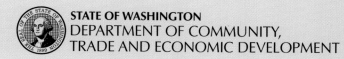

Destination Development, Inc. (DDI) is the leading tourism and resort development consulting firm in North America. Assisting both public-sector entities and privately developed projects, the award-winning DDI team has become a one-stop-shop for virtually all tourism/resort development and marketing projects. Services include the creation of Tourism Development & Marketing Plans, site planning (resorts, golf course communities, etc.), attractions development, architecture, landscape architecture, downtown and resort revitalization, Main Street programs, branding and repositioning programs, theme development, wayfinding and signage programs, cultural arts and facilities planning, and a host of other tourism and resort-related services.

The Washington State Office of Community, Trade and Economic Development (CTED), is charged with enhancing and promoting sustainable economic vitality throughout Washington state. From services and manufacturing to tourism, CTED works in partnership with businesses, communities, local economic development organizations, and tribes to attract, retain, expand, and support economic activity that promotes prosperity and improves the quality of life throughout the state. CTED's Economic Development Division delivers a wide range of services–from assisting with complex permitting processes to infrastructure and business financing, education and training, and marketing the state as a premier tourist destination and desirable place to live and work.